UNOFFICIAL DOCUMENTS OF THE

DEMOCRACY MOVEMENT IN COMMUNIST CHINA

1978-1981

中 國 民 主 運 動 資 料

UNOFFICIAL DOCUMENTS OF THE

DEMOCRACY MOVEMENT IN COMMUNIST CHINA

1978-1981

中 國 民 主 運 動 資 料

A Checklist of Chinese Materials in the Hoover
Institution on War, Revolution and Peace

compiled by I-mu

依 牧 編

East Asian Collection

Hoover Institution

Stanford, California

1986

The Hoover Institution on War, Revolution and Peace, founded at Stanford University in 1919 by the late President Herbert Hoover, is an interdisciplinary research center for advanced study on domestic and international affairs in the twentieth century. The views expressed in its publications are entirely those of the authors and do not necessarily reflect the views of the staff, officers, or Board of Overseers of the Hoover Institution.

Hoover Press Bibliography 67

© 1986 by the Board of Trustees of the Leland Stanford Junior University

All rights reserved. No part of this publication may be reproduced, stored in a retrieval system, or transmitted in any form or by any means, electronic, mechanical, photocopying, recording, or otherwise, without written permission of the publisher.

First printing, 1986

Manufactured in the United States of America

90 89 88 87 86   9 8 7 6 5 4 3 2 1

Library of Congress Cataloging in Publication Data

Hoover Institution on War, Revolution and Peace.
  Unofficial documents of the Democracy Movement in Communist China, 1978-1981 = Chung-kuo min chu yun tung tzu liao / compiled by I-mu.

  (Hoover Press bibliographical series ; 67)
  English and Chinese.

  1. Underground literature--China--Bibliography--Catalogs. 2. Hoover Institution on War, Revolution and Peace--Catalogs. I. I-mu. II. Title: Chung-kuo min chu yun tung tzu liao. III. Series.
Z3108.U5H66 1986   016.95105´7   86-7616
[PN5367.U5]
ISBN 0-8179-2672-0 (pbk.)

CONTENTS
目　錄

Foreword
前　言

A Review of Collections
文 集 內 容 淺 釋

Chronological Events of the Democracy Movement
民 主 運 動 紀 事

Min pan k'an wu
民 辦 刊 物

    1. Journals
       期 刊

    2. Pamphlets
       小 冊 子

    3. A Selection of Democracy Wall Papers
       民 主 牆 大 字 報 文 選

Claude Widor Collection: Unofficial Journals Published
  Outside Peking
華 達 存 集 : 民 辦 刊 物 北 京 外 地 出 版

A Collection of Underground Publications:
  Circulated on the Chinese Mainland, Compiled by David
  Goodman
大 陸 地 下 刊 物 彙 編

List of Chinese Unofficial Publications of the
  "Democracy Movement" 1978-1980, Compiled by the Institute
  for the Study of Chinese Communist Problems, Taipei
中 國 民 主 運 動 資 料

FOREWORD

In China the Communist Party completely dominates and imposes its will. Even the death of Mao Tse-tung on September 19, 1976, did not alter that state of affairs. But on November 23, 1978, a unique event occurred that signalled a momentous challenge to the Chinese Communist Party (CCP): Lü P'u placed a newsletter on a wall in Peking.

Why should the publication of a private newsletter be of such significance? In October 1949, the CCP had proclaimed the founding of the People's Republic of China. Lü wanted to inform the public of some new facts and interpretations, information unavailable to the people because of the rigid controls exercised by the CCP.

Lü named and criticized Mao Tse-tung's mistakes, and tried to explain why a great public demonstration had taken place on April 5, 1976, in T'ien-an-men Square of the country's capital. Lü claimed the people had become fed up with conditions in the country. He blamed the CCP for poor management of the economy and for stifling all criticism of the Party.

In subsequent months Lü's brave act was duplicated by many others who also circulated their privately printed pamphlets, wall posters, and perhaps most important of all, journals not authorized by the CCP. The contents of these documents told much about life and conditions in China and scathingly criticized the governance of the CCP. Some of this literature even appealed for more free expression and for the CCP to relax its controls over society.

These publishing activities did not last for very long. By April 1981 the Party's Central Committee was calling for greater discipline and warning the membership to refrain from supporting its critics. By the spring of 1982 most of the activists who had engaged in these publications had been arrested and imprisoned.

The Hoover Institution has made vigorous efforts to collect all documents pertinent to this important period in China and to preserve them for future use. This checklist of the Hoover Institution's holdings provides a convenient reference guide for those wishing to search out relevant materials that might elucidate and interpret the thought and action of those who spoke out so candidly about life and conditions in Communist China.

                                        Ramon H. Myers
                                        Curator-Scholar
                                        East Asian Collection

A REVIEW OF COLLECTIONS

文 集 內 容 淺 釋

The Collections are divided into four parts as follows:

A. <u>Min</u> <u>pan</u> <u>k'an</u> <u>wu</u> (民辦 刊物) was compiled by I-mu.

This collection contains 70 unofficial Chinese journals, 32 pamphlets and 28 items of Democracy Wall papers. The materials were collected from five sources. They are either in mimeographed form or xeroxed copies of mimeographs. The majority of them are from Mr. Nigel Wade, a reporter for the London <u>Daily</u> <u>Telegraph</u>, and comprise 29 journals and 10 pamphlets. Mr. Wade received the original copy of Wei Ching-sheng's (魏京生) autobiography from Yang Kuang (楊光) before Wei was arrested in Peking on March 29, 1978. Wei was sentenced to fifteen years in prison.

One of the items is his handwritten English translation of Yang Kuang's personal love story. Mr. Wade's careful calligraphy reflects his own respect for the sincerity and devotion of these young people, who anticipated that in promoting democracy and the legal system for their country they might lose their lives. Yet they believed that they must pay the price for the best interests of their country.

The second group of materials was received from Mr. Fu Pao-shih (傅葆石). It contains 16 journals and 7 pamphlets. Most of his collection was gathered after the arrest of Wei Ching-sheng, from late 1979 to September 1980.

We also acquired some material from Mr. Wang Tsai-sheng (王載生) and Ms. Ch'en Jo-hsi (陳若曦), and from Mr. Harold Richter of the West German Embassy during his work in Peking.

The materials are arranged alphabetically according to the Wade-Giles romanization.

The 70 titles and the issues of the journals can be retrieved in the RLG/CJK system by searching under the local subject heading Minpan k'anwu, or under the Chinese character string 民辦 刊物.

Titles and issues that appear in David Goodman's microfilm collection but that are not duplicated in our printed journals, are included in the holdings of this group of materials. The same practice is applied to the <u>Ta lu ti hsia k'an wu hui pien</u> (大陸地下刊物彙編), published in

Taipei.

B. <u>Claude Widor Collection: Unofficial journals published outside Peking.</u>

This collection contains 67 journals, totaling more than 200 issues; 60 percent are originals, 40 percent xerox copies. The journals themselves originate from 21 cities, the major ones being Canton, Shanghai, Hanzhou, Changsha, Wuhan and Tianjin.

They were published in the years 1979-1980, with a peak in 1980, the year when the focus of the Democracy Movement shifted from the capital, where it had been stifled, to the provinces. The provincial journals illustrate this later phase of the Democracy Movement, characterized by the formation of a nationwide grouping of all unofficial publications, and by the participation of Democracy activists in local direct elections.

C. <u>List of Chinese unofficial publications of the "Democracy Movement," 1978-1980</u>, collected by David Goodman.
Oxford : Bodleian Library, 1981. 3 microfilm reels.

This microfilm collection contains 49 titles: 27 journals and 22 miscellanea. The microfilm is randomly sequenced. An alphabetical list of Pinyin sequence is attached to the beginning of the first reel. There are a few notes under some titles.

Microfilm of the collection can be purchased from the Department of Oriental Books of Oxford's Bodleian Library.

D. <u>Ta lu ti hsia k'an wu hui pien</u> (大陸地下刊物彙編) [A collection of the underground publications: Circulation on Chinese mainland]. Taipei : The Institute for the Study of Chinese Communist Problems, 1980-1983. 15 vols.

This collection contains reprints of 25 journals and miscellaneous items.

Sequence of the collection:
Most of these journals were published irregularly. Collectors in Taipei could not always acquire these materials immediately upon publication. The material was grouped randomly. Titles of the journals are listed in alphabetial sequence with their issue and volume number

(when available) and date of publication.

Table of contents:

Many of the original journals did not have a table of contents when published. This collection has provided a table of contents at the beginning of each volume, which has made the collection easier to use. A pink sheet of the original journal was inserted before the printed copy.

Limitations on editing:

Since private publication was not allowed in the People's Republic of China, the places of publication of the original mimeographs were kept in semi-secrecy. Papers, inks and printing equipment were not available for unofficial publication; in addition, most of the journals were published by workers who did not have previous publishing experience.

During the reprinting of this collection, characters that could not be figured out with certainty have been noted in parentheses; unrecognizable characters have been identified by ▱ . This notation questions the reliability of the text without providing any suppositions. Chung-kuo ta lu ti hsia wen hsüeh mu lu （中國大陸地下刊物目錄）

[Catalog of Chinese underground literature] was edited and published by the same institution. The two-volume table of contents in Chinese and English covers most of the Institution's collection.

E. <u>Chung-kuo min pan k'an wu hui pien</u> (中国民办刊物彙编) [Documents on the Chinese democratic movement] 1978-1980, compiled by Claude Widor. Paris : L'Ecole de Hautes Etudes en Sciences Sociales, 1981- . v. 1-2. C-DS779.15.W5.

These two volumes are part of a projected six-volume series. A preface and introduction in French, English and Chinese describe the background and history of the Democracy Movement as well as some of the organizational changes that occurred when materials were being published.

CHRONOLOGICAL EVENTS

OF THE DEMOCRACY MOVEMENT

民 主 運 動 紀 事

1974

Nov. 10　Li I-che (李一哲) wall paper appeared on Pei-ching Road in Canton. The 67 pages of the wall paper focused on : (1) Damage to the citizens caused by bureaucratic corruption of the Chinese Communist Party (CCP) during the ten years of the Cultural Revolution; and (2) The need to practice democracy and a legal system in China.

1976

Jan. 8　Chou En-lai died.

Apr. 5　The T'ien-an-men Incident in Peking ended with heavy casualties. The theme of the incident was the need to end feudalistic rule. This incident was called the April 5th Movement.

Apr. 7　Mao Tse-tung proposed that the Politburo of the Central Committee of the CCP denounced Teng Hsiao-p'ing's (邓小平) official positions and that Hua Kuo-feng (华国锋) would assume Teng's positions as prime minister of the State Council and the vice-chairman of the CCP. The committee adopted both proposals.

Sept. 9 Mao Tse-tung died.

Oct. 6 Hua Kuo-feng, supported by Yeh Chien-ying (葉劍英), Li Hsien-nien (李先念), and other members of the Politburo arrested the Gang of Four. On the following day, Hua was voted in as chairman of the CCP and chairman of the Central Military Committee by a joint meeting of the First Secretaries of the Provincial Party Committees and the Politburo of the Central Committee of the CCP.

Oct. 22 Hua was inaugurated at T'ien-an-men.

1977

Feb. 7 Hua Kuo-feng and Wang Tung-hsing (汪東兴) instructed the Editorial Boards of <u>Jen min jih pao</u> (人民日报), <u>Chieh fang chün pao</u> (解放軍报) and <u>Hung ch'i</u> (紅旗) to publicize in their editorials that they would honor Mao's policy and his instruction to the full extent.

July 21 During the 3rd Plenary Session of the CCP's 10th Central Committee, Teng Hsiao-p'ing resumed his positions as prime minister of the State Council and vice-chairman of the CCP.

Aug. 18 The 11th National Congress of the CCP recommended

adding the "Four Great Freedoms" (四大自由) to Article 45 of the Constitution.

1978

Spring The remaining 130,000 victims of the anti-right wing movement, who had been removed from their positions in 1957, recovered their social status.

May The movement to promote the slogan: "Pragmatism is the standard in measuring truth" marked the key difference between Teng and Hua.

June-July Wall papers were widely spread on campuses.

Sept. Foreign journalists reported that they were allowed free contact with Chinese people. This report was reproduced in <u>Ts´an k´ao tzu liao</u> (参考資料).

Oct. 1 "To liberate thought, to provide the best service to the people are the duties of CCP members" -- this theme for the CCP Party was posted on Hsi-tan Wall in Peking by civilians.

People were gradually allowed to post their opinions and free-style literature on street walls throughout the country.

Nov. 15 The city government of Peking announced that activists in the Tien-an-men Incident were innocent. This was confirmed by the Central Committee of the CCP on Dec. 7 and officially announced by the 3rd Plenary of the 11th Congress of the CCP on December 22.

Nov. 22 It was estimated that over 100,000 people gathered at the People's Square in Shanghai. This demonstration called for a check and balance political system for China.

Nov. 23 Lü P'u (呂樸) posted his writings on Democracy Wall in Hsi-tan. He criticized Mao Tse-tung and pointed out that the real reasons behind the April 5th Movement were a backward economy, rigid thought control, and the poor living conditions of the people. Ta-tzu Pao (大字報) was called the "Fire Lighter of Democracy Wall".

Nov. 25 The Democracy Assembly Group was formed by Jen Wan-t'ing (任畹町) and eight other youths. Two days later they gathered at Hsi-tan Democracy Wall and led a public march to Tien-an-men Square. Over 10,000 participants demanded democracy and human rights for China. This date marks the beginning of the Democracy Movement.

Nov. 26 Vice-chairman Teng told the Japanese delegates of the Democratic-Socialist Party that, according to the Constitution, the Democracy Wall activities were legal. But Teng noted that some party comrades did not want to criticize Mao, and he agreed.

Nov. 29 <u>Ch´i meng</u> (啓蒙), the first unofficial publication, appeared in Kuei-yang (貴陽). Later it was reprinted in Peking in January 1979.

Dec. 5 "The fifth modernization--democracy and others" written by Wei Ching-sheng (魏京生), was posted on Democracy Wall. This long article strongly criticized the undemocratic practices of Mao and Teng. It also emphasized that (1) the history of Germany, Russia and China proved that anti-democracy was the cause of the poor living conditions of the people; and (2) the political system of Yugoslavia would be a good model for bringing economic wellbeing to the people.

Dec. 13 "To liberate thought, practice pragmatism; together we look forward to a better future." This was Teng´s statement to the Central Work

Conference of the CCP. He emphasized that in the past decade:

1. The government had enforced false Marxism to restrict people's thought;
2. The bureaucracy had smothered the initiative of most people since major problems were handled by only a few leaders;
3. The people had lost incentive for merit, since unrewarded good workers tended to be jealous of rewarded people;
4. The government had refused new technology.

The above speech provided the basis for the theme of the 3rd Plenary Session of the CCP's 11th Central Committee.

Dec. 16 <u>Ssu</u> <u>wu</u> <u>lun</u> <u>t'an</u> (四五論壇), a moderate unofficial journal, published its first issue.

Dec. 22 The communique of the 3rd Plenary Session of the CCP's 11th Central Committe announced the following national political guidelines:

1. The CCP doctrines were to be based on socialism, proletarian dictatorship, CCP leadership, Marxism, Leninism and Maoism;
2. Equality before the law;

3. Glorifying individual achievement was to be avoided;

4. Pragmatism should be the standard of government policy;

5. The Special Case Committees were to be dissolved and replaced by the Central Organization Bureau.

1979

Jan. 1 The United States, under the Carter administration, officially recognized China.

Jan. 8 In memory of the 3rd anniversary of Chou En-lai's death Fu Yüeh-hua (傅月華), a laborer of Peking, joined a march of hundreds of peasants and "sent-down" (下放) youths, who returned to the city from many provinces to demonstrate against hunger and purge and to plead for human rights. The march expanded to include fifty thousand participants and spectators. During that month, seven of them died of winter chill and hunger, and the masses protested in front of the government building in Chung-nan hai (中南海).

Jan. 15 Six leading unofficial journals announced their

intention of fighting for the basic constitutional rights: freedom of speech and freedom of the press without retaliation.

Jan. 18 Fu Yüeh-hua was arrested by the Security Bureau of Peking for disrupting public order and security.

Jan. 22 In the editorial of the *Jen min jih pao,* "To accelerate and strengthen the agricultural development policy," the writer reflected that a national effort should be made to improve the poor living conditions of the peasants, who composed 80 percent of the population.

Jan. 28 The members of seven unofficial journals in Peking organized a Joint Conference to counter the criticism against their literature on Democracy Wall. These members met weekly to discuss recent public issues.

Jan. 28 -Feb. 5 Teng Hsiao-p'ing visited the United States. An agreement was signed during the visit to open consulates in the United States.

Feb. 5 The "sent-down" youths of Shanghai rushed back to the city to claim job assignments. Since their requests were not granted, they protested at the government offices, broke into violent

	fights, sat on train tracks, and blocked traffic. During this period, the same situation occurred in Yünnan.
Feb. 8	The Joint Meeting of Unofficial Journalists investigated legal grounds for the arrest of Fu by the Police Department.
Feb. 12 & 15	The legal system was discussed by the editorials of the Jen min jih pao. These two articles emphasized the need to arrest those who criticized the government and those who were seeking personal gain by using the slogan "DEMOCRACY".
Mar. 20	"We request the government to reinstate the position of Head of the State" was posted on Democracy Wall by Chou Chien-min (周建民) and Chao Hsiao-min (趙小民). The poster suggested that Teng should be head of state and that state and party should be divided, democratic elections should be held for government officers, and party cadres should be selected by election and examination.
Mar. 22	"Human rights is not a proper slogan for the proletarian" was stated in the Pei-ching jih pao (北京日报).

Mar. 25 Wei Ching-sheng opposed Teng's decision to arrest the activists of the Democracy Movement and wrote and published the article "Do we want democracy or new dictatorial Marxism?" in T'an so hao wai (探索号外), Peking. This article attacks Teng's statement (released on March 16), which reconfirmed that "Without Mao Tse-tung, there is no New China; the CCP will be guided by Mao's thought." Wei ideologically refused to accept Teng's policy that suppressing the Democracy Movement by arresting the activists was for the good of the people. Wei urged the Chinese people not to trust Teng blindly.

Mar. 29 "The Announcement of the Peking Revolution Committee" adopted six guidelines to prevent statewide disorder. The last of these prohibited any political attacks on communist rule. Wei and some members of unofficial journals were arrested the same day.

Mar. 30 At the Conference of the Cadre of the CCP Teng Hsiao-p'ing clarified the Four Firm Guidelines (四堅持) set by him for interpreting the government policy, which were socialism, proletarian dictatorship, CCP leadership, Marxism and Maoism. He also severely criticized: (1) people who complained in a letter to President Carter about human rights violations of individuals; and (2) activities of the Democracy Movement and the demonstrations calling for anti-hunger measures and for human rights in Peking and Shanghai.

Apr.　　<u>Pei-ching</u> <u>chih</u> <u>ch'un</u> (北京之春), no. 4 listed the names of 23 activists of the April 5th Movement.

Apr. 1　The Central Government decided upon new policies regarding wall papers and demonstrations. A wall-cleaning campaign was carried on in all major cities, except Hsi-tan.

Apr. 3　Fu's family received the official arrest notice from the Peking Public Security Bureau after she had been kept in the Bureau for over two and a half months.

Apr. 4　On the night before the third anniversary of the April 5th Movement, thousands of petitioners were confined in Wu-ch'i Cadre School (五七干校), and Jen Wan-t'ing was arrested.

May　　"Human rights should be called the citizen's

rights in Chinese expression," was noted by Shih Hua-sheng (石撐生) in <u>Ssu wu lun t'an</u>, no. 9.

Foreign journalists in Peking, who had privately contacted the activists of the Democracy Movement, were labeled as international spies during the Conference of the Peking Security Bureau.

July 1 The 5th National People's Congress, 2nd Plenary Session, accomplished the following matters:
1. The drafts of seven major national laws were passed, effective January 1, 1980;
2. The new election system was established for selecting public officers;
3. The system for local government operation was decentralized and the direct election system was expanded to the district level;
4. Forty percent of workers in the nation were to get wage increases;
5. Younger civil workers were to be recruited.

These were the banners that this new leadership used to promote the pragmatic modernization of China.

Aug. 26 <u>Ssu wu lun t'an</u> organized a public debate on the theme "Democracy." The meeting started with a public opinion poll on the pros and cons of the arrest of three Democracy Movement activists. About a thousand people attended. This activity was a breakthrough toward democracy on the grass-roots level.

Sept. The poor had surged to Peking from all provinces; they were, for example, CCP members, war veterans, poor peasants, and "sent-down" students. Chairman Hua instructed the Central Government to send out over one thousand officers to help these people. The officials of the Central Government used a large building to provide free food and shelter for the poor. In many cases, the officers accompanied the victims back to their home towns and tried to assist them in regaining their jobs. Some of them resided temporarily along the Yung-ting River.

Sept. 8 Lu Lin (路林) replaced Wei Ching-sheng as chief editor of T'an so (探索). The journal declared that its main concern was to find the cause of the backward living conditions in China.

Sept. 29   The police department in Peking confiscated the artworks of the Hsing-hsing Art Exhibition (星星美展). On October 1, this organization led a parade and carried flags with such slogans as "Protect the Constitution," "Plead for democracy," and "Freedom for artists and their works." They won the conflict with the police department, and the paintings were returned to them. The Peking Art Association also promised to help them with their exhibition on November 1.

Oct.   Current political journals published in Hongkong were censored in China.

Oct. 6   Wei Ching-sheng's trial took place in Peking Court.

Oct. 10   Students of People's University participated in the parades and class strikes against the long-term use of campus buildings for military units or factory spaces since the Cultural Revolution. The People's Liberation Army returned the People's University campus to the People's University the following spring.

Oct. 14   Following the above example, the demonstrators asked the First Military Medical University to return the Chi-nan University campus to its original owner. Liao Ch´eng-chih (廖承志) instructed the former to vacate ten percent of the campus space in favor of its owner. But the rest was retained until the students of Chi-nan University demonstrated again in December 1981.

Oct. 15　Wei Ching-sheng was sentenced to fifteen years in prison. The ruling was partly based on the Punitive Regulation of a Counter Revolutionist. Wei argued that he did not know about the existence of this regulation, which was dated 1951.

Oct. 17　Fu Yüeh-hua´s case was tried in public, but the case was thrown into turmoil when she provided dramatic evidence of her innocence.

Oct. 22　The editorial of <u>Jen min jih pao</u> analyzed the administrative practices of the government for handling the upsurge of petitioners in Peking. It outlined for the masses the correct strategy for handling this problem. The two points were: (1) avoid using demonstrations; and (2) try to settle employment issues at the local level to avoid wasting money and time in coming to

Peking.

Nov. 2 Teng made a speech referring to this editorial about the upsurge of petitioners. He emphasized that the officers who were dealing with these problems must use flexible methods.

Nov. 10 The theme of the 4th Plenary Session of the CCP's Central Committee (四中全会) was to enforce the Four Firm Guidelines. Teng Hsiao-p'ing emphasized that the current democracy-human rights movements was aimed not only against Mao Tse-tung, but against the CCP. Chao Tzu-yang (趙紫陽), governor of Szechwan, emphasized in the <u>Jen min jih pao</u> that in order to avoid interference with "thought liberation" for the four modernizations and to ensure CCP leadership, he opposed the unlimited capitalism in China. According to P'eng Ch'ung (彭冲), mayor of

Shanghai, the shaky situation of the CCP leadership in China was caused by:

1. Overuse of the leftist line in the Party;
2. Poor living conditions;
3. Mistakes caused by the government and the Party;

opportunists.

Kuo Lo-chi (郭羅基) challenged Chao's article. Four days later, in the same newspaper, Kuo responded that "freedom is very precious for mankind. It is not the exclusive property of capitalists."

Nov. 11 About 100 police officers and plain-clothes secret police officers appeared at the Hsi-tan Democracy Wall. Three youths were arrested because they distributed the record of the trial of Wei Ching-sheng. Liu Ch'ing (刘青) went to Peking Public Security, explaining that he was responsible for the availability of the record. He was then arrested and the three others were released.

Nov. 29 The Decision of the People's Congress stated that the citizens of Peking should only post wall papers at Yüeh-t'an Park, which replaced the Hsi-tan Democracy Wall. Writers of the wall papers had to register their names and service units with the officers before posting. The effective date was December 8.

Dec. 7 This was the last day for wall papers on Hsi-tan Wall.

1980

Jan. 16 Teng's speech, "Current conditions and responsibilities," to the Cadre Meeting of the CCP stressed that:

1. Hsi-tan Democracy Wall and its activity caused social instability. Those Democracy Movement activists believe that socialism is not compatible with capitalism and that China is not better than Taiwan. Individualism and disturbing the social order are factors causing the state's instability and social unrest. These activities should be handled seriously.

2. The Four Firm Guidelines were being successfully carried out by the offices of the different government departments in cooperation with the Security Verification Committee of each department.

3. "The right to speak out freely, air their views fully, hold great debates, and write wall papers (大字报)" -- the so called Big Four (四大) listed in Article 45 of the Constitution -- had never functioned

effectively. Teng announced that he would present this view to the People's Congress and that the opinion of the majority should provide grounds to eliminate them from the Constitution.

4. Military force could supplement local security in case of local riots.

5. In the past three years, 2.9 million cases of victims of the political movements had been reversed -- not including the victims of the T'ien-an-men Incident.

6. The government had added 7 million jobs to the workforce in the past year.

Apr.-Nov. The election for the district representatives of the New First Session of the National People's Congress was enforced.

The students of major universities such as Peking University, Ts'ing-hua University, Ch'ang-sha Normal College, and Wu-han and Cheng-chou Universities, promoted the local democratic election. During the campaign, some students emphasized that they were non-CCP members and did not support the Four Firm Guidelines. It happened that these candidates were the ones who won the election. Although the government intended to improve their political system, they could not afford to run the risk of discrediting the CCP.

Some of the Democracy activists were elected as the local representatives on campuses and in local factories, but a few were disqualified by the local authorities because of their outspoken speeches. Fu Shen-ch'i (傅申奇) of Shanghai and Wang Yi-feng (王屹峯) of Ch'ing-wan (清宛), Hopeh were two examples.

In Changsha, students carried on hunger strikes, public demonstrations, and classroom sit-ins to protest the interference of the Party in the final election process. They sent 32 delegates to Peking on November 1.

In general, the students viewed this open district election as the cornerstone for reforming the civil service system of the Chinese government.

July Liu Ch'ing was sentenced to two years in prison. He was sent to Shensi.

Aug. Liao Kai-lung (廖蓋隆), member of the Policy Office of the CCP, initiated the Keng-sheng

Reformation Proposal. He emphasized that "Democracy is the means and a goal." This proposal called for China to imitate the structure of the Polish government and to have direct elections at the hsien (県) level. It was rejected by the representatives at the 6th Plenary Session of the 11th Central Committee of the CCP in August 1981. They believed that such drastic change could harm the stability of the state.

Aug. 28- Sept. 12 The 5th National People's Congress of PRC, 3rd Session, was held. The four major changes stemming from this Congress were:

1. The leadership of China intended to separate the government administration from the CCP. Chao Tzu-yang was elected premier of the newly formed State Council, while Hua Kuo-feng resigned from his post. Seven deputy premiers were added to the new department.

2. Criticism of the government should be tolerated so long as it does not affect the image of the national leaders and the stability of the socialist state.

3. Many cities started to re-establish legal offices, which had been closed down since 1967.

4. On September 10, one of the delegates proposed revising Article 45 of the Constitution. By the end of the Congress 3,220 out of 3,400 representatives voted to revise the Constitution and to eliminate Article 45. The new Constitution would be effective as of January 1981.

Sept. 21   <u>Tse jen</u> (責任) appeared, a journal published by the newly formed Association of National Chinese Unofficial Journals (中华全国民刊協会) in Canton.

Oct.   The National Publishing Bureau in Peking proposed to the State Council to legalize the unofficial publications. The proposal was shelved by the State Department.

Nov.   <u>Che i tai</u> (這一代) was a joint effort of the students of thirteen Chinese language and journalism departments of major universities, who formerly published their own journals. The editors of the original journals rotated turns on the editorial board. The first issue was published by Wu-han University.

Students of major colleges and universities petitioned for new "Publication Laws."

Nov. 14　Hsü Wen-li (徐文立) stated his support for the Poland labor organization Solidarity.

Nov. 16　An officer of Peking City visited Ts'ui Ch'üan-hung (翟全洪) and informed him that leaders of the Peking Government were working on a general policy regarding unofficial publications.

Dec.　The Shanghai Security Bureau released a few dozen Democracy activists after keeping them imprisoned for over one and a half years.

The Central Committee of the CCP held a Work Conference on Stability and Economic Growth of the State. There was a general consensus that individual liberties stirred up unrest in the state.

1981

Jan.　The central government criticized the Changsha authorities for their interference in the election process.

Jan. 16　<u>Hung ch'i</u> published an article, "Opposing

	liberalization," reflecting the dissatisfaction of the higher cadre.
Feb.	Fu Yüeh-hua was released from jail. She was then set to a labor camp.
Feb. 8	The editorial of the <u>Jen min jih pao</u> stated that the national democratic innovations should be gradually carried out, but only on the condition of national unification and stability. People should avoid using public petitions, declarations, labor strikes, and sit-ins, for example, in the name of democracy and freedom. This editorial is based on document no. 2 of the CCP released in January.
Mar.	The ninth document of the Central Committee of the CCP focused on:

1. Ceasing the activities of Democracy activists;
2. CCP members losing their membership by assisting or contacting Democracy activists;
3. Provincial Party Committees in the nation strengthening their efforts to clean up local political chaos by focusing on the citizens who were against the Four Firm Guidelines and eliminating the illegal

organizations or people who read publications released by Democracy activists.

Apr. 5 Three hundred participants gathered from different parts of China to celebrate the fifth anniversary of the April 5th Movement. Twenty-four editors of the democracy journals from all provinces were arrested during April.

Apr. 15 <u>Jen min jih pao</u> attacked the wall paper activities, expressing the wish to limit freedom of speech and freedom of the press.

May 26 The Central Committee of the CCP decided that Democracy journals were to be censored; college journals, even when they were supported by the provincial CCP, were also to cease publication.

June <u>Che jen</u> published its last issue. This ended the free publication and Democracy Movement in China.

Sept. 1 The deputy minister for foreign affairs stated at a press conference in Peking that foreign correspondent should neither contact Chinese political activists nor report their activities and publications to the correspondents' employers.

Sept. 14 Liu Ch'ing released his report on his life in jail to the foreign reporters. This action brought him an additional seven years of prison.

1982

May 28 Wang Hsi-che (王希哲) was sentenced to fourteen years of prison.

May 29 Ho Ch'iu (何求) was sentenced to ten years of prison.

June 8 Hsü Wen-li (徐文立) was sentenced to fifteen years and the length of the sentences varied for the rest of the editors.

Aug. 27 At the National Conference of Publication for Youth in Peking Wang Jen-chung (王任重) criticized the unofficial publications that spoke against the Four Firm Guidelines.

Sept. 1 "Strengthen the criticism of literature," an article in Hung-ch'i (紅旗), confirmed the importance of the Four Firm Guidelines and Mao's thought.

Nov. 17 In order to revive the Democracy Movement, Wang Ping-chang's (王炳章) Spring of China Movement started in New York.

MIN PAN K'AN WU

民办刊物

1. JOURNALS
   期 刊

(Che i tai)

这 一代. (武昌：武汉 大学 中文系)

    no. 1, Nov.1979

Vault
C-DS
779.15
M45
no.52

(Ch'i meng)

启蒙. ([贵阳，北京]：启蒙社)

    no. 1-2, Oct-Nov.1978

Vault
C-DS
779.15
M45
no.2

(Ch'i meng)

启蒙. (北京：启蒙社 北京 分社)

    no. 1-2, Jan-Mar.1979

Vault
C-DS
779.15
M45
no.3

A difference of opinion caused the split of the Editorial Board of the Association of Ch'i ming. In early 1979, Li Chia-hua published another edition of Ch'i meng.

(Ch'i meng ts'ung k'an)

启蒙 丛刊. (贵阳：启蒙社)

    v. 1-5, Nov.1978-Mar.1979

Vault
Mic.
C-DS
779.15
M451
no.11

(Ch'iang)

墙. ([北京：秋实 编辑部])

    no. 1, Nov.1979

Vault
Mic.
C-DS
779.15
M451
no.37

(Chieh tung)
解凍. (北京：解凍社)

    no. 1-9, Jan.1979-May 1980

Vault
Mic.
C-DS
779.15
M451
no.4

(Chih chiang)
之江. (杭州：杭州 之江 雜誌社)

    no. 1-2, Sept-Nov.? 1980

Vault
C-DS
779.15
M45
no.4

(Chih hsin)
志新. (北京：志新詩社)

    no. 1, Oct.1979

Vault
C-DS
779.15
M45
no.5

(Chin t'ien)
今天. ([北京]：今天 編輯部)

    no. 1-3, 5-6; Dec.1978-May 1979;
      no. 4, 7-9; 1979-1980 in <u>Ta lu ti hsia
      wen hsüeh k'an wu hui pien</u>, v. 7, 9-11.

Vault
C-DS
779.15
M45
no.6

(Ch'iu shih)
秋实. (北京：秋收 編輯部)

    no. 1, Mar.1979; no. 4-5, Aug-Sept.1979;
      no.2, Apr.1979 on Mic. no.9;
      no.3, July 1979 in <u>Ta lu ti hsia k'an
      wu hui pien</u>, v. 6.

Vault
C-DS
779.15
M45
no.7

(Ch'iu shih pao)

求是 报. (北京：出版者 缺)

    no. 1-2, 4, 6, 11, 14, 16; Jan-Oct.1979
      (printed copy);
      no. 5, 7-10, 12, 15, 17; Mar-Dec.1979
      on Mic. no.35

Vault
C-DS
779.15
M45
no.8

(Ch'iu so)

求索. (北京：[求索 诗社])

    no. 1, Feb.1979

Vault
C-DS
779.15
M45
no.51

(Ch'u hang)

初 航. ([北京：北京 師范 大学])

    no. 2, Jan.1979; no.5, Oct.1979

Vault
C-DS
779.15
M45
no.49

(Chü hsing)

聚星. ([重慶：出版者 缺])

    no. 1, Dec.? 1980

Vault
C-DS
779.15
M45
no.9

(Ch'üan min ko ch'ü)

全民 歌曲. ([北京：全民 歌曲 編輯部])

    no. 1-3, Mar-Apr.1979

Vault
C-DS
779.15
M45
no.10

(Chui hsün)

追寻. ([Madison, New York : Wei Kuo])

    no. 1-2, Jan-Mar.1983;
      no.4, Jan.1984

C-DS
779.15
C384

(Ch'un chung ts'an k'ao hsiao hsi)
群众 参考 消息. ([北京] : 北京 大学)

    no. 1-6, Dec.1978-Apr.1979

Vault
C-DS
779.15
M45
no.11

(Ch'un t'ien)
春天. (太原 : 山西 大学 学生会)

    no. 1, Dec.1979

Vault
C-DS
779.15
M45
no.50

(Chung-kuo chih ch'un)
中国 之 春. ([New York] : 中国之春編輯部)

    no. 1, Dec.1983-

C-AP
95.C4
C4854

(Chung-kuo chih sheng)
中國 之 聲 (Rego Park, New York : 國聲出版社)

    no. 1, Sept.1983-

C-DS
779.15
C385

(Chung-kuo jen ch'üan)
中国 人权. (北京 : 中国 人权 同盟)

    no. 1, Feb.1979;
      no.2, Mar.1979 in <u>Ta lu ti hsia k'an wu hui pen</u>, v.3.

Split into two factions after no. 1; another edition initiated by Jen Wan-t'ing.

Vault
C-DS
779.15
M45
no.12

(Chung-kuo jen ch'üan)

中国 人权. ([北京] : 中国 人权 同盟)

    Mar.1979; no.4 and suppl., Mar-Apr.1979
       in <u>Ta lu ti hsia k'an wu hui pien</u>, v. 1.

Vault
C-DS
779.15
M45
no.13

(Chung sheng)

钟 声. (武汉 : 四 五 学会)

    no. 1, June 1979; no. 4-5, Apr-July 1980

Vault
C-DS
779.15
M45
no.14

(Feng fan)

风 帆. (太原 : 风帆 编辑部)

    no. 1, Dec.1980

Vault
C-DS
779.15
M45
no.15

(Feng yeh)

枫葉. (北京 : 海天區 文化馆)

    Added title: 海天文艺

    no. 1, Mar.1979; no.3, May 1979;
      no. 6, Sept.1979 (printed)

Vault
Mic.
C-DS
779.15
M451
no.39

(Hai lang hua)

海浪 花. (青岛 : 青岛 工人 同人 刊物社)

    no. 1, 3, 10, Aug.1979-Dec.1980;
      Hao wai, Nov.1980

Vault
C-DS
779.15
M45
no.16

(Hai yen)
海燕. (上海 : 出版者 缺)

    no. 4-5, 1979

Vault
C-DS
779.15
M45
no.53

(Hsin she hui)
新 社会. (香港 : 文化新潮社及左翼評論)

    no. 2-3, Oct.1980-Mar.1981

C-HX
9
H7

(Hsin shih hsüeh)
新 詩學. (貴州 : 解凍 社)

    no. 3, Mar.1979

Vault
C-DS
779.15
M45
no.17

(Hsin t'ien ti)
新 天地. (北京 : 中美人民友好报社)

    no. 1, Mar.1977

Vault
C-DS
779.15
M45
no.18

(Hsüan chü chien pao)
选举简报. (上海 : 傅申奇)

    no. 6-8, 10-11; May 20-28, 1980

Vault
C-DS
779.15
M45
no.18.1

(Hsüeh hsi t'ung hsün)
学習 通訊. (北京 : 徐 文立)

    no. 4-5, Oct-Nov.1980

Vault
C-DS
779.15
M45
no.19

(Hsüeh yu t'ung hsin)
学友 通信. (广州：人民之路 雜誌社)　　　　　Vault
　　　　　　　　　　　　　　　　　　　　　　　　C-DS
　　　　　　　　　　　　　　　　　　　　　　　　779.15
　　　　　　　　　　　　　　　　　　　　　　　　M45
  no. 11, Nov.1980 (including Mao Tse-tung yü no.20
   wen hua ta ko ming);
   no. 1, 5; Feb.1980 in <u>Ta lu ti hsia k'an wu</u>
   <u>hui pien</u>, v. 14.

(Hua tz'u)
花刺. (北京：出版者 缺)　　　　　　　　　　Vault
　　　　　　　　　　　　　　　　　　　　　　　　Mic.
　　　　　　　　　　　　　　　　　　　　　　　　C-DS
　　　　　　　　　　　　　　　　　　　　　　　　779.15
  no. 1, Apr.1979   M451
　　　　　　　　　　　　　　　　　　　　　　　　no.40

(Huo hua)
火花. (北京：火花 編辑社)　　　　　　　　　Vault
　　　　　　　　　　　　　　　　　　　　　　　　Mic.
　　　　　　　　　　　　　　　　　　　　　　　　C-DS
　　　　　　　　　　　　　　　　　　　　　　　　779.15
  no. 1, Mar.1979   M451
　　　　　　　　　　　　　　　　　　　　　　　　no.41

(I shu yü k'o hsu"eh chien hsün)
艺术 与 科学 简讯. (北京：出版者 缺)　　　　Vault
　　　　　　　　　　　　　　　　　　　　　　　　C-DS
　　　　　　　　　　　　　　　　　　　　　　　　779.15
　　　　　　　　　　　　　　　　　　　　　　　　M45
  Sept.1979   no.21

(Jen min chih sheng)
人民 之声. (广州：广州 科学 社会 主义 学会; Vault
 人民 之声 編辑部)   C-DS
　　　　　　　　　　　　　　　　　　　　　　　　779.15
　　　　　　　　　　　　　　　　　　　　　　　　M45
  no. 3-13, Feb-Dec.1979;   no.22
   Special no. 2, Dec.1980

(K'o hsüeh min chu fa chih)
科学 民主 法制. (北京：中国 戏曲 学院)

    no. 1-16, Jan-June 1979

Vault
Mic.
C-DS
779.15
M451
no.6

(K'uang piao)
狂飚. ([北京]：狂飚 書屋)

    no. 1, Sept.1979

Vault
Mic.
C-DS
779.15
M451
no.23

(Kung ho pao)
共和 报. (長沙：新中 机械厂)

    no. 5, Dec.1980

Vault
C-DS
779.15
M45
no.23

(Li hsiang t'ung hsün, kung ho pao t'e k'an)
理想 通訊, 共和 报 特刊. (長沙：湖南 师范 学院)

    no. 1-2, Oct.1980

Vault
C-DS
779.15
M45
no.24

(Li lun ch'i)
理論 旗. ([北京：出版者 缺])

    no. 2, Sept.1980

Vault
C-DS
779.15
M45
no.25

(Lun jen ch'üan)
論 人权. (北京, 貴陽：启蒙社)

    no. 3, Jan.1979

Vault
C-DS
779.15
M45
no.26

(Min chu ch'iang)
民主牆. (北京：民主牆 雜誌 編輯 委員会)

    Dec.1978

Vault
C-DS
779.15
M45
no.27

(Min chu chih sheng)
民主 之 声. (上海：中华 全国 民刊 協会)

    no. 8-9, Nov.1980;
       no. 4, Nov.1980 (Hao wai : Keng shen
       pien fa)

Vault
C-DS
779.15
M45
no.28

(Min chu t'ao lun)
民主 讨论. (上海：民主 讨论会)

    no. 1, Mar.1979

Vault
C-DS
779.15
M45
no.54

(Min chu yü shih tai)
民主 与 时代. (北京：民主 与 时代 編辑部)

    no. 1, Mar.1979

Vault
C-DS
779.15
M45
no.29

(Min hsin)
民心. (橫浜 : 中国民主团結联盟日本分部)

    no. 2-3, Dec.1983-Jan.1984

Vault
C-DS
779.15
M45
no.29.1

(Nei pu chien pao)
内部 简报. ([北京]：中国 人权 同盟 秘书组)

    no. 2, Mar.1979

Vault
Mic.
C-DS
779.15
M451
no.47

(Pai hua)
百花．（[北京]：百花 編輯部）

    no. 1-2, Sept-Nov.1979

Vault
C-DS
779.15
M45
no.30

(Pei-ching chih ch'un)
北京 之 春．（北京：北京 大学）

    no. 1-6, 8-9; Jan-Nov.1979;
      no.7, Aug.1979 in <u>Ta lu ti hsia k'an
      wu hui pien</u>, v. 8.

Vault
C-DS
779.15
M45
no.31

(Pei-ching ch'ing nien)
北京 青年．（北京：苏誼）

    no. 2, Jan.1981

Vault
C-DS
779.15
M45
no.32

(Po chung)
播种．（[Alhambra, Ca.： 播种編輯部]）

    no. 1, Sept.1983-

C-DS
779.15
P662

(P'u kung ying)
蒲公英．（北京：出版者 缺）

    no. 2, 4, 6; Feb-June 1979

Vault
Mic.
C-DS
779.15
M451
no.38

(Sheng huo)
生活．（广州：出版者 缺）

    no. 1, Apr.1979; no. 4, Dec.1979

Vault
C-DS
779.15
M45
no.33

(Shih tai)
時代. (北京：出版者 缺)

    no. 1, Oct.1979;
      no. 2, Oct.1979 on Mic. no.15

Vault
C-DS
779.15
M45
no.34

(Shih yü ch'ao)
時 与 潮. (北京：出版者 缺)

    no. 1, Oct.1979

Vault
Mic.
C-DS
779.15
M451
no.16

(Ssu hua lun t'an)
四化 論坛. (北京：出版者 缺)

    no. 1, Sept.1979

Vault
C-DS
779.15
M45
no.35

(Ssu wu lun t'an)
四 五 論坛. (北京：四 五 論坛 編輯部)

    no. 2-10, 12-16, Dec.1979-Feb.1980;
      no. 1, Jan.1978 and no.11, July 1979 on
      Mic. no.34;
      no. 17 in <u>Ta lu ti hsia k'an wu hui pien</u>,
      v. 11.
      no. 2 incomplete.

Vault
C-DS
779.15
M45
no.36

(Ssu wu pao)
四 五 报. (杭州：四 五 学会)

    no. 1, Nov.1978;
      no. 4, Apr.1979 on Mic. no.25

Vault
C-DS
779.15
M45
no.37

(Ta chü)
大局. (北京：出版者 缺)

    no. 1, Oct.1979

Vault
C-DS
779.15
M45
no.38

(T'an so)
探索. (北京：出版者 缺)

    no. 1-5, Dec.1978-Oct.1979

Vault
C-DS
779.15
M45
no.40

(T'an so)
探索 (Brooklyn, New York： 出版者 缺)

    no. 1, May 1983

C-DS
779.15
T31

(Ta hsüeh sheng t'ung hsün)
大学生 通訊. (武昌：武汉 大学)

    no. 2, Nov.1980

Vault
C-DS
779.15
M45
no.39

(Tse jen)
責任. (广州市, 上海：中华 全国 民刊 協会)

    no. 1-5, Sept.1980-Feb.1981

Vault
C-DS
779.15
M45
no.1

(Wei lai)
未來. ([廣州：廣州 地區 高等 文科 学生
《未來》 編輯部])

    no. 1, Mar.1979; no. 4, Apr.1979

Vault
C-DS
779.15
M45
no.46

(Wei ming hu)
未名湖. ([北京 : 北京 大学 五四 文学社])　　　　　Vault
　　　　　　　　　　　　　　　　　　　　　　　　　　　C-DS
　　　　　　　　　　　　　　　　　　　　　　　　　　　779.15
　　　　　　　　　　　　　　　　　　　　　　　　　　　M45
　　no. 1, Mar.1980　　　　　　　　　　　　　　　　　no.47

(Wen i pai chia)
文艺 百家. (出版地 缺 : 出版者 缺)　　　　　　　　　Vault
　　　　　　　　　　　　　　　　　　　　　　　　　　　C-DS
　　　　　　　　　　　　　　　　　　　　　　　　　　　779.15
　　　　　　　　　　　　　　　　　　　　　　　　　　　M45
　　no. 2, 1979 (incomplete)　　　　　　　　　　　　no.41

(Wo men)
我們. ([杭州 : 杭州 師範 学院 中文系])　　　　　　　Vault
　　　　　　　　　　　　　　　　　　　　　　　　　　　C-DS
　　　　　　　　　　　　　　　　　　　　　　　　　　　779.15
　　　　　　　　　　　　　　　　　　　　　　　　　　　M45
　　no. 1, 3; Sept.1979　　　　　　　　　　　　　　　no.42

(Wo men)
我們. (北京 : 馬文和)　　　　　　　　　　　　　　　Vault
　　　　　　　　　　　　　　　　　　　　　　　　　　　C-DS
　　　　　　　　　　　　　　　　　　　　　　　　　　　779.15
　　　　　　　　　　　　　　　　　　　　　　　　　　　M45
　　no. 1-2, Mar-June 1979　　　　　　　　　　　　　no.48

(Wo t´u)
沃土. (北京 : 李 嘉文)　　　　　　　　　　　　　　　Vault
　　　　　　　　　　　　　　　　　　　　　　　　　　　C-DS
　　　　　　　　　　　　　　　　　　　　　　　　　　　779.15
　　　　　　　　　　　　　　　　　　　　　　　　　　　M45
　　Feb-Oct.1979 (Oct.1979 has two editions);　　　no.43
　　　　Feb.1979 in <u>Ta lu ti hsia k´an wu hui pien</u>;
　　　　Suppl. no. 3, Nov.1979

(Yüan shang ts'ao)　　　　　　　　　　　　　　　　Vault
原　上　草．(北京：出版者　缺)　　　　　　　　　　C-DS
　　　　　　　　　　　　　　　　　　　　　　　　779.15
　　　　　　　　　　　　　　　　　　　　　　　　M45
　　no. 2, Mar.1979 (in memory of April 5th Move-　no.44
　　　　ment's third anniversary);
　　　　no. 1, Mar.1979 on Mic. no.19.

(Yüeh hai lou)　　　　　　　　　　　　　　　　　　Vault
月　海　楼．(北京：出版者　缺)　　　　　　　　　　C-DS
　　　　　　　　　　　　　　　　　　　　　　　　779.15
　　　　　　　　　　　　　　　　　　　　　　　　M45
　　no. 1, Sept.1979;　　　　　　　　　　　　　　 no.45
　　　　no. 2-3, Sept-Oct.1979 on Mic. no.20.

2. PAMPHLETS

小 冊 子

(Chi t´a yen tsou fa)
吉他演奏法

(Chi t´a yen tsou ko ch´ü)
吉他演奏歌曲

(Chia t´ing tsai nan -- she hui t´an t´ao)
家庭灾难－－社会探讨　手抄印本　傅申奇

(Chiao chi wu t´u p´u)
交际舞图谱

(Chih tsui kao jen min fa yüan chang Chiang Hua t´ung chih,
　　tsui kao jen min chien ... Huang Huo-ch´ing t´ung chih
　　ti kung k´ai hsin)
致最高人民法院长江华同志最高人民检查院检查长黄火青同志的公开信　付月华家上
　　1979.2.28

(Chü sang ti hui ku yü chan wang)
沮丧的回顾与瞻望　　刘青　作　1981.6

(Chung-hua jen min kung ho kuo ch´u pan yin shua fa hsing fa
　　(ts´ao an))
中华人民共和国出版印刷发行法(草案)

(Chung-kuo jen ch´üan hsüan yen 19 t´iao)
中国人权宣言　19条　　中国人权同盟　1979年1月于北京

(Chung-kuo jen ch´üan t´ung meng chih hsing wei yüan hui
　　hui i)
中国人权同盟执行委员会会议　1979.2.27

(Chung-kuo jen ch'üan t'ung meng chih hsing wei yüan hui kuan yü shao shu jen ... fen lieh ti chüeh i)
中国人权同盟执行委员会关于少数人盗用同盟名义公开分裂的决议   1979.2.27

(Fei pao ti chi tien)
菲薄的祭奠　甲必円　1979

(Fu Yüeh-hua shih chien kei kung an, chien ch'a, ssu fa teng yu kuan pu men ti i feng kung k'ai hsin)
付月华事件给公安,检查,司法等有关部门的一封公开信   1979.2.19

(Hsia Hsün-chien kei Nai-chieh-erh Wei-te ti hsin)
夏训健给奈杰尔·韦德的信   1979.3.23

(Hsü Shui-liang chi)
徐水良集   1980

(Hu-nan shih yüan min chu hsüan chü)
湖南师院民主选举   1980.9.23-1980.11.13
　　　介绍侯选人陶森　湖南师院中文系77,78级下分选民联合调查整理
　　　民主选举全过程　　　　请愿记实（湖南师院选举民意代表团
　　　全体绝食同学给同学们的信　（湖南师院全体绝食同学）
　　　告全国各兄弟院校书　湖南师院请愿总代表团
　　　长沙特讯：　湖南师院学生为捍卫民主权利而斗争
　　　往北京团情况通报（湖南师院请愿代表团）

(I hsüan chü chih tu kai ko k'an jen min tai piao ta hui chih tu)
以选举制度改革看人民代表大会制度

(I shu hsiao tz'u tien)
艺术小辞典

(Kao ch'üan shih jen min shu)
告全市人民書　1980.10.15

(Ko ch'ü)
歌曲

(Ko ming cheng ch'üan chi ch'i tsai Chung-kuo ti shih chien)
革命政权及其在中国的实践　惠君　1979.3

(Kuang-chou min k'an "Jen min chih sheng" li ch'ang shu)
广州民刊"人民之声"立場書

(Kung kao)
公告　(星星)露天美术展览会　1979.9.29

(Lun li shih jen wu tui li shih ti tso yung yü fan tso yung)
論历史人物对历史的作用與反作用　黃翔　著　1979.3.19

(Lun wu ch'an chieh chi min chu ko ming (hsüeh shu) t'ao lun)
論无产阶级民主革命(学术)讨论.　陈尔晋　(北京：四五 论坛 编辑部)
　　1979

(Pao hu kuo chia k'uang shan, wan hui ching chi shun shih, fa
　　chan she tui ch'i yeh)
保护国家矿山；挽回経済損失，發展社队企业　周大计　1979.1

(Pei ts'an ti tsai yü, ts'an k'u ti tou cheng, p'ao chuan yin
　　yü chi)
悲惨的遭迂，殘酷地鬥爭，抛砖引玉集　麒麟

(Shih k'o hsüeh she hui chu i ma)
是科学社会主义嗎？

(Shih wo ya, tzu yu shen)
是我啊：自由神！春丝作　1979.3.2

(Teng Li-chün ko chi)
邓丽君 歌集　第一集

(Ts'ung shou hai che tao pu hsin che)
从受害者到不幸者　1979.2

(Tui kung ch'an chu i she hui ti she hsiang)
对共产主义社会的设想　克向作

(Yang yü)
阴郁　扬光著　1979.2.26

3. A SELECTION OF DEMOCRACY WALL PAPERS

民 主 牆 大 字 報 文 選

(Ch´i su shu)
起訴書(第一号) 中国科学院一〇九厂公民团 1978.11.18

(Ch´iang lieh yao ch´iu shih ching wei jen chen kuan ch´e
　　Kuo wu yüan 166 hao wen chien)
强烈要求市經委认真貫彻国务院166号文件 中央財政金融学院教职員
　　1978.11.22

(Chieh fang ssu hsiang, ming pien chen li)
解放思想，明辨真理

(Chieh wu pu liang li, ko ming mo kou ch´ieh)
揭捂不兩立·革命莫苟且 --評吳德-- 1978.10.5
　　　　Incomplete

(Chih ch´i meng she)
致啓蒙社
　　　　Incomplete

(Chih ch´ih ch´i su)
支持起訴：北京天线電仪四厂 陳銘邨 1978.11.21

(Chih Chung kung Chung yang "Jen min jih pao" she kung
　　k´ai hsin)
致中共中央"人民日报"社公开信 1978
　　　　Incomplete

(Chih k´ung chün hou pu Tang wei ti kung k´ai hsin)
致空軍后部党委的公开信 李东 1978.11.20

(Chih tang Chung yang, Hua chu hsi, Chung yang chün wei, Kuo
　　wu yüan ti i feng kung k´ai hsin)
致党中央华主席．中央軍委，国务院的一封公开信 立理德 1978.12.26

(Chih tang Chung yang kung k'ai hsin)
致党中央公开信　王樂文　1978.10

(Ch'ing wen, wen hua ta ko ming kei wo men tai lai to shao hao ch'u)
請问‧文化大革命給我们帶來多少好处？　1978.11.18

(Fa lü ho hsien tai hua)
法律和现代化　　1978.11.29
　　　Poor printing

(Fa yang "ssu wu" ko ming ching shen chiang ko ming chin hsing tao ti)
發揚"四五"革命精神將革命进行到底　民益　1978.11.21

(Fei shuo pu hsing)
非説不行　1978.11

(Hsin yüan)
心愿〈二〉,〈三〉
　　　Incomplete

(I tien i chien)
一点意見　老实人　1978.11.29

(Jih chi chi tse)
日記几則　吾非吾　1978.9-1978.11

(Kung min t´ung hsün -- chih Mei-kuo Chi-mi K´a t´e tsung t´ung)
公民通訊--致美国吉米卡特总统　　中国"人权小组"　1978.12.7

(Lei li feng hsing chua, chih cheng chao hsi kuei min yüan)
雷历风行抓　只争朝夕归民冤　李靖吉　1978.11.28

(Lun Mao Tse-tung ti kung kuo)
论毛泽东的功过　　董思东

(Min chu ch´iang san ying)
民主牆散影

(Min chu pi hsü shen p´an tu ts´ai)
民主必须审判独裁　　吴文　1978

(Pan k´ai pan chiao shih, hsiang hsien tai hua chin chün -- chih Wang Tung-hsing)
撇开绊脚石, 向现代化进军--致汪东兴　公一民　1978.11.25

(Shang fang che ti hu yü shu)
上訪者的呼吁書

(T´ao Chu li ying p´ing fan)
陶铸理应平反　　小民　1978.11.24

(Tsai t´an)
再談　捍卫　1978.11.25

65

(Tsung li ch'üeh tsai hsüeh chung shui)
总理却在雪中睡 甲必丹 1978.11.16

(Wo men ti k'an fa ho hu yü)
我们的看法和呼吁

CLAUDE WIDOR COLLECTION: UNOFFICIAL JOURNALS
PUBLISHED OUTSIDE PEKING

華達存集：民辦刊物北京外地出版

(Ch'ao)
潮．（保定：出版者 缺）   Vault C-DS 779.15 M452 no.1

   no. 1-2, Nov.1979-Feb.1980

(Che-chiang chih ch'un)
浙江之春．（杭州：《浙江之春》编辑部）   Vault C-DS 779.15 M452 no.2

   no. 1, Sept.1979

(Ch'en chung)
沈钟．（杭州：《沈钟》杂志社）   Vault C-DS 779.15 M452 no.3

   no. 1-2, Jan-Mar.1979

(Ch'i ming hsing)
启明星．（武汉：钟声杂志社）   Vault C-DS 779.15 M452 no.4

   no. 1, Sept/Oct.1979;
     no. 3-4, Oct.1979-May 1980

(Chih chiang)
之江．（杭州：之江杂志社）   Vault C-DS 779.15 M452 no.5

   no. 1-2, Sept-Nov.1980

(Chih chiang chih ch'un)
之江之春．（杭州：《之江之春》编辑部）   Vault C-DS 779.15 M452 no.6

   no. 1, Sept.1979

(Chih yu lun t´an)
志友 论坛. (青岛 : 《志友 论坛》 编辑部)　　Vault C-DS 779.15 M452 no.7

    no. 1, Nov.1980

(Ching nü)
静女. (桂林 : 广广, 宇平, 悟提)　　Vault C-DS 779.15 M452 no.8

    no. 1, Nov.1980

(Chüeh ch´i ti i tai)
崛起 的 一代. (贵阳 : 贵州 大学 中文系)　　Vault C-DS 779.15 M452 no.9

    no. 1-2, Nov-Dec.1980

(Chung sheng)
钟声. (武汉 : 四 五 学会)　　Vault C-DS 779.15 M452 no.10

    no. 1-7, July 1979-Dec.1980

(Fa)
筏. (上海 : 上海 戏剧 学院)　　Vault C-DS 779.15 M452 no.11

    no. 2, Oct.1979

(Fei tieh)
飞碟. (宁波 : 国民 刊 协会)　　Vault C-DS 779.15 M452 no.12

    no. 1-2, Sept-Nov.1980

(Fei tieh k'uai pao)

飞碟 快报 （付刊）．（武汉 ： 出版者 缺）
續 "野草"

    no. 1, May 1980

Vault
C-DS
779.15
M452
no.13

(Feng fan)

风帆．（太原 ：《风帆 人民 之 声》编辑）

    no. 1, Dec.1980

Vault
C-DS
779.15
M452
no.14

(Hai lang hua)

海浪 花．（青島 ： 海浪 花 编辑部）

    no. 1-10, Aug.1979-Dec.1980;
       Suppl. no. 1, June 1980

Vault
C-DS
779.15
M452
no.15

(Hai yen)

海燕．（上海 ： 出版者 缺）

    no. 10, Jan.1981

Vault
C-DS
779.15
M452
no.16

(Hou ch'i chih hsiu)

后起 之 秀．（上海 ： 魯弟 青年 文艺社）

    no. 1, June 1980

Vault
C-DS
779.15
M452
no.17

(Hsi tso yüan ti)

習作 园地．（太原 ： 青年 业余 学习 小组）

    no. 1, Aug.1980

Vault
C-DS
779.15
M452
no.18

(Hsi tso yüan ti)
習作 园地. (開封 : 出版者 缺)

    no. 7-12, July-Oct.1980

Vault C-DS 779.15 M452 no.19

(Hsia li pa jen)
下里巴 人. (哈尔浜 : 《下里巴 人》编辑部)

    no. 1, Mar.1979

Vault C-DS 779.15 M452 no.20

(Hsiao hsi pao tao)
消息 報導. (貴陽 : 啓蒙社 編輯社, 使命 編輯部)

    no. 1-2, Oct-Nov.1980

Vault C-DS 779.15 M452 no.21

(Hsiao tzu pao)
小字报. (重庆 : 小字报 筹备組 印)

    no. 1, Oct.1979

Vault C-DS 779.15 M452 no.22

(Hsin ch'ing nien)
新青年. (上海 : 中华 全国 民刊 協会)

    no. 3, Dec.1980; special issue, 1980

Vault C-DS 779.15 M452 no.23

(Hsin chüeh wu)
新 覺悟. (天津 : 《新 覺悟》 编辑部)

    no. 1, Mar.1979

Vault C-DS 779.15 M452 no.24

(Hsin shih tai)
新 时代. (安陽 : 《新 时代》编辑部)

    no. 1-3, Oct.1979-Mar.1980;
       Suppl., Dec.1979

Vault
C-DS
779.15
M452
no.25

(Hsing kuang)
星光. (安陽 : 《星光》编辑部)

    no. 1-4, Oct.1980-Jan.1981

Vault
C-DS
779.15
M452
no.26

(Hsüeh shu t'ao lun)
学术 讨论. (天津 : 出版者 缺)

    July-Sept.1980

Vault
C-DS
779.15
M452
no.27

(Hsüeh yu t'ung hsin)
学友 通信. (广州 : 人民 之 路 雜誌社)

    no. 1, 3-5, 7; June-Nov.1980

Vault
C-DS
779.15
M452
no.28

(Hua hsia ch'un)
华夏 春. (万県 : 四川华夏春编辑部)

    no. 1-2, Oct-Dec.1982

Vault
C-DS
779.15
M452
no.29

(Hua tung min k'an)
华东 民刊. (杭州 : 《之江》,《飞碟》,
    《民主 之 声》 合办)

    no. 1, Jan.1981

Vault
C-DS
779.15
M452
no.30

(Jen chien)

人間. (宁波 : 人間 文学社)

    no. 1, Feb.1980

Vault
C-DS
779.15
M452
no.31

(Jen min chih lu)

人民 之 路. (广州 : 《人民 之 路》 编辑部)

    no. 1-7, Sept.1979-Oct.1980
       newsletter : Apr.1980

Vault
C-DS
779.15
M452
no.32

(Jen min chih sheng)

人民 之 声. (广州 : 广州 科学 社会 主义)

    no. 1-13, Jan-Dec.1979;
      special issue no. 2, Dec.1980

Vault
C-DS
779.15
M452
no.33

(Kung ho pao)

共和 報. (長沙 : 出版者 缺)

    no. 1-2, Mar-May 1980; no. 5, Dec.1980

Vault
C-DS
779.15
M452
no.34

(Lang hua)

浪花. (广州 : 出版者 缺)

    no. 1-2, Aug-Nov.1979

Vault
C-DS
779.15
M452
no.35

(Li hsiang t'ung hsün)

理想 通訊. (長沙 : 基礎 大学 图書館)

    no. 1-2, 4; no. 5-7, Sept-Dec.1980

Vault
C-DS
779.15
M452
no.36

(Li lun ch'i)
理论 旗. (青岛 : 鲁基)

    no. 1-2, Sept-Nov.1980

Vault
C-DS
779.15
M452
no.37

(Liu lang che)
流浪者. (長沙 : 《流浪者》 编辑部)

    no. 3-6, Apr-Nov.1979

Vault
C-DS
779.15
M452
no.38

(Mei kuei)
玫瑰. (杭州 : 《玫瑰》 编辑部)

    no. 1, 1980

Vault
C-DS
779.15
M452
no.39

(Min chu chih sheng)
民主 之 声. (上海 : 《民主 之 声》 编辑部)

    no. 3-9, Aug-Nov.1980;
      extra issues : no. 1-4, Sept-Nov.1981;
      no. 6, Jan.1981

Vault
C-DS
779.15
M452
no.40

(Min chu chuan)
民主 磚. (安陽市 : 《民主 磚》 编辑部)

    no. 1-7, Oct.1979-Nov.1980;
      extra issue : Jan.1981

Vault
C-DS
779.15
M452
no.41

(Min chu yü fa chih pao)
民主 与 法制 報. (錦州 : 出版者 缺)

    no. 1-2, 1979; no. 4, Feb.1979

Vault
C-DS
779.15
M452
no.42

(Min sheng)
民声（《春丛》付刊）. (長沙市 : 魯迅 学社)

    no. 2-3, [no date];
      no. 4-6, 9-10, 12, Oct-Dec.1979

Vault
C-DS
779.15
M452
no.43

(Ming t´ien)
明天. (賓陽市 : 《童音》 啟蒙社 编辑部
   联合 出版)
    no. 1, Jan. 1981

Vault
C-DS
779.15
M452
no.44

(Ni ch´ung yeh t´an)
泥虫 野潭. (上海 : 出版者 缺)

    no. 2-3, Jan.1981

Vault
C-DS
779.15
M452
no.45

(Pei chiang)
北江. (韶关市 : 出版者 缺)

    no. 1-2, May-July 1980

Vault
C-DS
779.15
M452
no.46

(P´ing lun)
評论. (天津市 : 《評论》 编辑部)

    no. 1-11, Mar.1979-Sept.1980

Vault
C-DS
779.15
M452
no.47

(Po hai chih pin)
渤海 之 滨. (天津市 : 《渤海 之 滨》 编辑部)

    no. 1, Sept.1979

Vault
C-DS
779.15
M452
no.48

(Sheng huo)
生活．（广州市：出版者 缺）

    no. 2-4, June-Dec.1979

Vault
C-DS
779.15
M452
no.49

(Sheng ssu chien)
生死 谏．（天津市：出版者 缺）

    1980

Vault
C-DS
779.15
M452
no.50

(Shih ming)
使命．（贵阳市：《使命》编辑部）

    no. 4, Jan.1980

Vault
C-DS
779.15
M452
no.51

(Shih yeh)
视野．（西安市：出版者 缺）

    no. 4, Sept.1979

Vault
C-DS
779.15
M452
no.52

(Shu sheng)
庶声．（韶关市：出版者 缺）

    no. 1-19, 21-22, 25, Jan-Dec.1980

Vault
C-DS
779.15
M452
no.53

(Shuang chou p'ing lun)
双周 评論．（贵阳市：出版者 缺）

    no. 15, [no date]; no. 19, Dec.1980;
       no. 22, [no date]

Vault
C-DS
779.15
M452
no.54

(Ssu k'ao)

思考. (杭州 : 浙江省 杭州 大学 政治系，历史系)

 no. 2, Nov.1979

Vault
C-DS
779.15
M452
no.55

(Ssu wu)

四 五. (杭州 : 《四 五》 杂志社)

 no. 4-11, Apr-Nov.1979

Vault
C-DS
779.15
M452
no.56

(Tse jen)

責任. (广州市，上海 : 中华 全国 民刊 協会)

 no. 1-4, Sept.1980-Jan.1981

Vault
C-DS
779.15
M452
no.57

(Tung t'ai)

动态. (长沙 : 《动态》 编辑部)

 1979; no. 3, 1980

Vault
C-DS
779.15
M452
no.58

(T'ung yin)

童音. (重慶市 : 《童音》 编辑部)

 1980

Vault
C-DS
779.15
M452
no.59

("Tzu yu t'an" fu k'an)

《自由談》 副刊. (广州市 : 《自由談》
 副刊 编辑部)

 no. 1, 1980

Vault
C-DS
779.15
M452
no.60

(Wei ming)

未名. (《未名》 編輯部)

    no. 1, Nov.1979

Vault
C-DS
779.15
M452
no.61

(Wo men)

我們. (杭州 : 杭州 師范 学院)

    no. 1-3, Mar-Sept.1979

Vault
C-DS
779.15
M452
no.62

(Wu ming)

无名. (開封 : 无名 文学社)

    no. 2, Sept.1980; no. 5, Dec.? 1980

Vault
C-DS
779.15
M452
no.63

(Wu shen)

无神. (武汉 : 武汉 大学 经济系 七八 年級)

    no. 1, 1980?

Vault
C-DS
779.15
M452
no.64

(Yen ching)

眼睛. (長春市 : 出版者 缺)

    no. 2, July 1980

Vault
C-DS
779.15
M452
no.65

(Yen chiu chien pao)

研究 簡报. (天津市 : 社会 科学 研究会)

    no. 1-2, Aug-Sept.1980

Vault
C-DS
779.15
M452
no.66

(Yüeh hui)　　　　　　　　　　　　　　　　　Vault
约会. (安阳市 : 出版者 缺)　　　　　　　　　C-DS
　　　　　　　　　　　　　　　　　　　　　779.15
　　no. 1, [no date]　　　　　　　　　　　M452
　　　　　　　　　　　　　　　　　　　　　no.67

A COLLECTION OF UNDERGROUND PUBLICATIONS

Circulated on the Chinese Mainland

大 陸 地 下 刊 物 彙 編

(Che-chiang chih ch'un)　　　　　　　　　　Vault
浙江之春．（杭州：《浙江之春》　　　　　　　C-DS
　　編輯部）　　　　　　　　　　　　　　　　779.15
　　　　no. 1, Sept.? 1979　　　　　　　　　T35C58
　　　　　　　　　　　　　　　　　　　　　　vol.15

(Ch'i meng)　　　　　　　　　　　　　　　　Vault
启蒙．（[貴陽，北京]：启蒙社，）　　　　　　C-DS
　　　　　　　　　　　　　　　　　　　　　　779.15
　　　　no. 1-2, Oct-Nov.1978　　　　　　　T35C58
　　　　　　　　　　　　　　　　　　　　　　vol.1

(Ch'i meng ts'ung k'an)　　　　　　　　　Vault
启蒙丛刊．（貴阳：启蒙社）　　　　　　　　　C-DS
　　　　　　　　　　　　　　　　　　　　　　779.15
　　　　v. 1-5, Nov.1978-Mar.1979　　　　　T35C58
　　　　　　　　　　　　　　　　　　　　　　vol.3

(Chin t'ien)　　　　　　　　　　　　　　　　Vault
今天．（[北京]：今天編輯部）　　　　　　　　C-DS
　　　　　　　　　　　　　　　　　　　　　　779.15
　　　　no. 1-9, Dec.1978-Mar.? 1980　　　T35C58
　　　　　　　　　　　　　　　　　　　　　　vol.4-11

(Ch'iu shih)　　　　　　　　　　　　　　　　Vault
秋实．（北京：秋实編輯部）　　　　　　　　　C-DS
　　　　　　　　　　　　　　　　　　　　　　779.15
　　　　no. 1-5, Mar-Sept.1979　　　　　　T35C58
　　　　　　　　　　　　　　　　　　　　　　vol.4-9

(Ch'iu shih pao)　　　　　　　　　　　　　Vault
求是报．（北京：出版者缺）　　　　　　　　　C-DS
　　　　　　　　　　　　　　　　　　　　　　779.15
　　　　no. 1-17, Jan-Nov.1979　　　　　　T35C58
　　　　　　　　　　　　　　　　　　　　　　vol.1-6

(Ch'ün chung ts'an kao hsiao hsi)
群众 参考 消息.（[北京]：北京 大学）

    no. 1-6, Dec.1978-Apr.1979

Vault
C-DS
779.15
T35C58
vol.1-4

(Chung-kuo jen ch'üan)
中国 人权.（[北京]：中国 人权 同盟）

    no. 1-3, Feb-Apr.1979
        Supplement, April 1979

Vault
C-DS
779.15
T35C58
vol.1-3

(Hsüeh yu t'ung hsin)
学友 通信.（广州：人民 之 路 雜誌社）

    no. 1-5, 1980

Vault
C-DS
779.15
T35C58
vol.14

(Huo hua)
火花.（北京：火花 編輯社）

    no. 1, Mar.1979

Vault
C-DS
779.15
T35C58
vol.5

(Jen min chih sheng)
人民 之 声.（广州：广州 科学 社会 主义
   学会；人民 之 声 編輯部）
    no. 3-7, Feb-June 1979;
      no. 9-10, Aug-Sept.1979

Vault
C-DS
779.15
T35C58
vol.1, 13-15

(K'o hsüeh min chu fa chih)
科学 民主 法制.（北京：中国 戏曲 学院）

    no. 1-12, Jan-May 1979

Vault
C-DS
779.15
T35C58
vol.6-15

(Lan feng)
嵐風. (北京 : 狂飈書屋)

    no. 1, Autumn 1979

Vault
C-DS
779.15
T35C58
vol.15

(Min chu chuan)
民主磚. (安陽 : 民主磚編輯部)

    no. 2, Nov.1979

Vault
C-DS
779.15
T35C58
vol.6

(Min chu yü shih tai)
民主 与 時代. (北京 : 民主 与 時代 編輯部)

    no. 1, Mar.1979

Vault
C-DS
779.15
T35C58
vol.2

(Nei pu ts'an k'ao)
內部 简报. ([北京] : 中国 人权 同盟 秘书組)

    no. 2, Nov.1979

Vault
C-DS
779.15
T35C58
vol.14

(Pai hua)
百花. ([北京] : 百花 編辑部)

    no. 1, Sept.1979

Vault
C-DS
779.15
T35C58
vol.13

(Pei-ching chih ch'un)
北京 之 春. (北京 : 北京 大学)

    no. 1-8, Jan-Sept.1979

Vault
C-DS
779.15
T35C58
vol.2-9

(Sheng huo)
生活. (广州：出版者　缺)

    no. 1, Apr.1979; no. 4, Dec.1979

Vault
C-DS
779.15
T35C58
vol.2, 12

(Shih tai)
時代. (北京：出版者　缺)

    no. 1-2, Oct.1979

Vault
C-DS
779.15
T35C58
vol.1, 12

(Ssu hua lun t'an)
四化　論坛. (北京：出版者　缺)

    no. 1, Sept.1979

Vault
C-DS
779.15
T35C58
vol.5

(Ssu wu lun t'an)
四　五　論坛. (北京：四　五　論坛　編輯部)

    no. 1, Dec.1978; no. 3-11, Jan-Aug.
      1979; no.13-15, Oct-Dec.1979;
      no. 17, Mar.1980

Vault
C-DS
779.15
T35C58
vol.1-11

(T'an so)
探索. (北京：出版者　缺)

    no. 1-5, Dec.1978-Oct.1979

Vault
C-DS
779.15
T35C58
vol.1-4

(Wo t'u)
沃土. (北京：李　嘉文)

    no. 1-5, Feb-Oct.1979

Vault
C-DS
779.15
T35C58
vol.10-13

(Yüan shang ts'ao)
原 上 草. (北京：出版者 缺）

    no. 1-2, Mar.1979

Vault
C-DS
779.15
T35C58
vol.13

(Yüeh hai yeh t'an)
粵海夜談. (广州 ： 中国变革问题研究小組）

    no. 1, May 1981

Vault
C-DS
779.15
T35C58
vol.15

LIST OF CHINESE UNOFFICIAL PUBLICATIONS OF

THE "DEMOCRACY MOVEMENT," 1978-1980

中國民主運動資料

(Bai hua)
百花. ([北京] : 百花 编辑部)

    no. 1-2, Sept-Nov.1979

Vault
Mic.
C-DS
779.15
M451
no.1

(Bei jing zhi chun)
北京 之 春. (北京 : 北京 大学)

    no. 1-6, Jan-June 1979; no. 8, Sept.1979

Vault
Mic.
C-DS
779.15
M451
no.2

(Bei jing zhi chun)
北京 之 春. (北京 : 北京 大学)

    no. 1, Mar.1979

Vault
Mic.
C-DS
779.15
M451
no.3

(Chen zhong)
沉钟. (杭州? : 《沉钟》杂志社)

    no. 1, Jan.1979

Vault
Mic.
C-DS
779.15
M451
no.24

(Dui gong chan zhu yi she hui de she xiang)
对共产主义社会的思想. (北京 : 求是报出版组)

    July 1979

Vault
Mic.
C-DS
779.15
M451
no.31

(Feng ye)

枫葉. (北京：海天區 文化馆)

    no. 1, Mar.1979; no. 3, May 1979

Vault Mic. C-DS 779.15 M451 no.39

(Ge ming zheng quan ju qi zai zhong guo de shi jian)

革命政权及其在中国的实践 / 惠 君. (北京：《求是报》出版卫)

    Mar.1979

Vault Mic. C-DS 779.15 M451 no.30

(Hua ci)

花刺. (北京：出版者 缺)

    no. 1-2, June-Aug.1979

Vault Mic. C-DS 779.15 M451 no.40

(Huo hua)

火花. (北京：火花 編輯社)

    no. 1, Mar.1979

Vault Mic. C-DS 779.15 M451 no.41

(I shi xiao ci dian)

艺術小辞典 / 旷 洋 执筆. (貴阳：[五青年畫展])

    Aug.1979

Vault Mic. C-DS 779.15 M451 no.27

(Jie dong)
解凍. (北京：解凍社)

    no. 3, Mar.1979

Vault
Mic.
C-DS
779.15
M451
no.4

(Jin Tian)
今天. ([北京]：今天 編輯部)

    no. 1-9, Jan.1979-May 1980

Vault
Mic.
C-DS
779.15
M451
no.5

(Ke xue min zhu fa zhi)
科学 民主 法制. (北京：中国 戏曲 学院)

    no. 1-16, Jan-June 1979

Vault
Mic.
C-DS
779.15
M451
no.6

(Kuang biao)
狂飚. ([北京]：狂飚 書屋)

    no. 1, Sept.1979

Vault
Mic.
C-DS
779.15
M451
no.23

(Minzhu qiang)
民主牆. (北京：民主牆 雜誌 編輯 委員会)

    Dec.1978

Vault
Mic.
C-DS
779.15
M451
no.7

(Min zhu yu shi dai)
民主 与 時代．(北京：民主 与 時代 編輯部)　　　Vault
　　　　　　　　　　　　　　　　　　　　　　　　　Mic.
　　　　　　　　　　　　　　　　　　　　　　　　　C-DS
　　　　　　　　　　　　　　　　　　　　　　　　　779.15
　　　　　　　　　　　　　　　　　　　　　　　　　M451
　　　no. 1, Mar.1979　　　　　　　　　　　　　　 no.8

(Pu gong ying)
蒲公英．(北京：出版者 缺)　　　　　　　　　　　Vault
　　　　　　　　　　　　　　　　　　　　　　　　　Mic.
　　　　　　　　　　　　　　　　　　　　　　　　　C-DS
　　　　　　　　　　　　　　　　　　　　　　　　　779.15
　　　　　　　　　　　　　　　　　　　　　　　　　M451
　　　no. 2, Feb.1979; no. 4, Apr.1979;　　　　　no.38
　　　　　no. 6, June 1979

(Qi meng)
启蒙．(北京：启蒙社北京分社)　　　　　　　　　Vault
　　　　　　　　　　　　　　　　　　　　　　　　　Mic.
　　　　　　　　　　　　　　　　　　　　　　　　　C-DS
　　　　　　　　　　　　　　　　　　　　　　　　　779.15
　　　　　　　　　　　　　　　　　　　　　　　　　M451
　　　no. 1-2, Jan-Mar.1979　　　　　　　　　　　no.36
　　　　　(no. 1 incomplete)

(Qi meng cong kan)
启蒙 丛刊．(貴阳：启蒙社)　　　　　　　　　　　Vault
　　　　　　　　　　　　　　　　　　　　　　　　　Mic.
　　　　　　　　　　　　　　　　　　　　　　　　　C-DS
　　　　　　　　　　　　　　　　　　　　　　　　　779.15
　　　　　　　　　　　　　　　　　　　　　　　　　M451
　　　no. 1-5, Nov.1978-Mar.1979　　　　　　　　 no.11

(Qiang)
墙．(北京：秋实編輯部)　　　　　　　　　　　　Vault
　　　　　　　　　　　　　　　　　　　　　　　　　Mic.
　　　　　　　　　　　　　　　　　　　　　　　　　C-DS
　　　　　　　　　　　　　　　　　　　　　　　　　779.15
　　　　　　　　　　　　　　　　　　　　　　　　　M451
　　　no. 1, Nov.1979　　　　　　　　　　　　　　 no.37

(Qiu shi)
秋实. (北京：秋实 編輯部)

    no. 1-2, Mar-Apr.1979;
      no.5 [n.d.]

Vault
Mic.
C-DS
779.15
M451
no.9

(Qiu shi bao)
求是 报. (北京：出版者 缺)

    no. 1-2, Jan-Feb.1979; no. 5-12,
      Mar-Aug.1979; no. 15-17, Oct-
      Nov.1979

Vault
Mic.
C-DS
779.15
M451
no.35

(Quan min ge qu)
全民 歌曲. ([北京：全民歌曲編輯部])

    no. 1-4, Apr-May 1979

Vault
Mic.
C-DS
779.15
M451
no. 12

(Qun zhong can kao xiao xi)
群众 参考 消息. ([北京]：北京 大学)

    no. 1-6, Dec.1978-May 1979

Vault
Mic.
C-DS
779.15
M451
no.42

(Ren min lun tan)
人民論壇. (北京？：出版者 缺)

    no. 1, Jan.1979

Vault
Mic.
C-DS
779.15
M451
no.13

(Ren min zhi sheng)　　　　　　　　　　　　　Vault
人民之声. (广州：广州科学社会主义学会；　　　Mic.
　　人民之声编辑部)　　　　　　　　　　　　C-DS
　　　　　　　　　　　　　　　　　　　　　　779.15
　　　　　　　　　　　　　　　　　　　　　　M451
　　　no. 3, Feb.1979　　　　　　　　　　　no.48

(Sheng huo)　　　　　　　　　　　　　　　　Vault
生活. (广州市：出版者　缺)　　　　　　　　　Mic.
　　　　　　　　　　　　　　　　　　　　　　C-DS
　　　　　　　　　　　　　　　　　　　　　　779.15
　　　　　　　　　　　　　　　　　　　　　　M451
　　　no. 1, Apr.1979　　　　　　　　　　　no.14

(Shi dai)　　　　　　　　　　　　　　　　　Vault
时代. (北京：出版者　缺)　　　　　　　　　　Mic.
　　　　　　　　　　　　　　　　　　　　　　C-DS
　　　　　　　　　　　　　　　　　　　　　　779.15
　　　　　　　　　　　　　　　　　　　　　　M451
　　　no. 1-2, Oct.1979　　　　　　　　　　no.15

(Shi dai de wei ren)　　　　　　　　　　　　Vault
时代的伟人 / 四五月刊評論員.　　　　　　　　Mic.
　　(北京？：[四五月刊社])　　　　　　　　　C-DS
　　　　　　　　　　　　　　　　　　　　　　779.15
　　　　　　　　　　　　　　　　　　　　　　M451
　　　Mar.1979　　　　　　　　　　　　　　　no.17

(Shi yu chao)　　　　　　　　　　　　　　　Vault
时与潮. (北京：出版者　缺)　　　　　　　　　Mic.
　　　　　　　　　　　　　　　　　　　　　　C-DS
　　　　　　　　　　　　　　　　　　　　　　779.15
　　　　　　　　　　　　　　　　　　　　　　M451
　　　no. 1, Oct.1979　　　　　　　　　　　no.16

(Shu xue bian zheng fa)
数学辨证法 / 王仑.（保定 : 出版者 缺）   Vault Mic. C-DS 779.15 M451 no.33

   [n.d.]

(Si wu)
四五.（杭州 : 四五杂志编辑部）   Vault Mic. C-DS 779.15 M451 no.25

   no. 4, Apr.1979

(Si wu lun tan)
四 五 論坛.（北京 : 四 五 論坛 編輯部）   Vault Mic. C-DS 779.15 M451 no.34

   no. 1-15, Dec.1978-Dec.1979

(Tan suo)
探索.（北京 : 出版者 缺）   Vault Mic. C-DS 779.15 M451 no.43

   no. 1-3, Dec.1978-Mar.1979;
     no. 5, Oct.1979

(Wei Jing-Sheng an jian shen li tao cheng)
魏京生案件勝利鬥争.（北京 : 商务）   Vault Mic. C-DS 779.15 M451 no.50

   Oct.1979

(Wo men)
我們. (杭州: 杭州 師範 学院)

    no. 3, Sept.1979

Vault
Mic.
C-DS
779.15
M451
no.26

(Wo tu)
沃土. (北京: 李 嘉文)

    Feb-Oct.1979

Vault
Mic.
C-DS
779.15
M451
no.18

(Xin tian di)
新 天 地. (北京: 中美 人民 友好 报社)

    no. 1, Mar.1979

Vault
Mic.
C-DS
779.15
M451
no.44

(Yuan shang cao)
原 上 草. (北京: 出版者 缺)

    no. 1-2, Mar.1979

Vault
Mic.
C-DS
779.15
M451
no.19

(Yue hai lou)
月 海 樓. (北京: 出版者 缺)

    no. 2-3, Sept.1979

Vault
Mic.
C-DS
779.15
M451
no.20

(Zhi xin)
志新. (北京：志新 詩社)

    no. 1, Oct.1979

Vault Mic. C-DS 779.15 M451 no.21

(Zhong guo ren quan)
中国 人权. ([北京]：中国 人权 同盟)

    no. 1, Feb.1979

Vault Mic. C-DS 779.15 M451 no.45

(Zhong guo ren quan)
中国 人权. ([北京]：中国 人权 同盟)

    no. 2, Mar.1979

Vault Mic. C-DS 779.15 M451 no.46

(Zhong guo ren quan)
中国 人权. (北京：中国 人权 同盟)

    In March 1979 the organization split into two factions.

    no. 3 and supplement, Apr.1979

Vault Mic. C-DS 779.15 M451 no.22

(Zhong guo ren quan tong meng: nei bu jian bao)
中国 人权 同盟：内卫简报. (北京：中国 人权 同盟)

    no. 2, Mar.1979

Vault Mic. C-DS 779.15 M451 no.47

(Zhong guo ren quan xuan yan)

中国 人权 宣言 / 中国 人权 同盟. ([北京] : 《《人权报》》印)

Jan.1979

Vault
Mic.
C-DS
779.15
M451
no.49